W9-BQW-125

OH, THE THINGS YOU CAN SAY FROM A-Z

LEARN ABOUT BIG AND LITTLE LETTERS

Adapted by Linda Hayward
and Cathy Goldsmith
from the works of

Dr. Seuss

SCHOLASTIC INC.   New York   Toronto   London   Auckland   Sydney

ISBN 0-590-67456-0

TM & © 1995 by Dr. Seuss Enterprises, L.P.
All rights reserved. Published by Scholastic Inc., 555 Broadway, New York, NY 10012, by arrangement with Random House, Inc.

12 11 10 9 8 7 6 5 4 3   6 7 8 9/9 0 1/0

Printed in the U.S.A.   14

First Scholastic printing, January 1996

First of all

there are some things
you should know.

I crossed it out.

 bit

I underlined it.

<u>it</u>   bit

I circled it.

   bit

I wrote it.

BIG A

little a

What can you say that begins with A?

Aunt Annie's alligator!

Underline all the big and little A's.

BIG B
little b

What can you say that begins with B?

Beetles battle in a bottle.

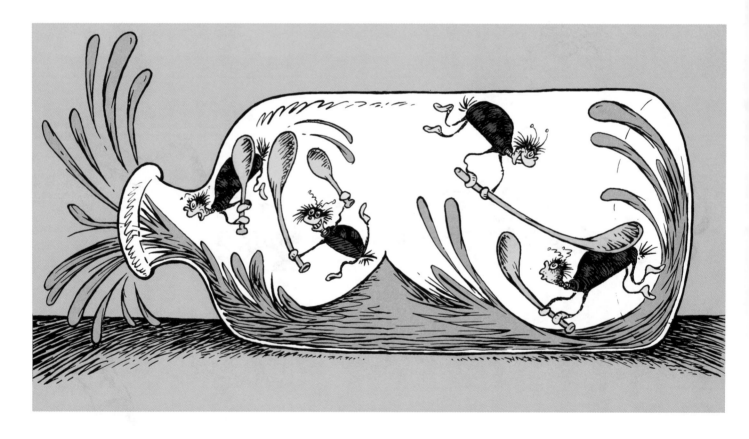

beetle   battle   bottle   alligator

Cross out the word that doesn't begin with B.

Color the big B's red.
Color the little b's blue.
Don't color the A at all.

How fast can you say this B word?

bubble

BIG C
little c

What can you say that begins with C?

Curious Crandalls come with candles.

Circle the C-shaped candle.

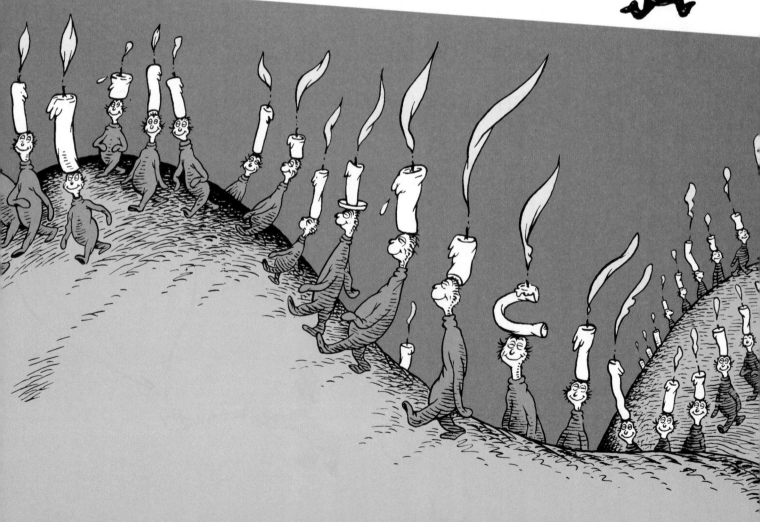

BIG D

little d

What can you say that begins with D?
David Donald Doo dreams of doughnuts.

Circle the D-shaped doughnut.

BIG E

little e

What do you see that begins with E?

Ellie's elegant elephant!

Draw a line
under each
and every E.

BIG F

little f

What can you say that begins with F?

Four fat fish!

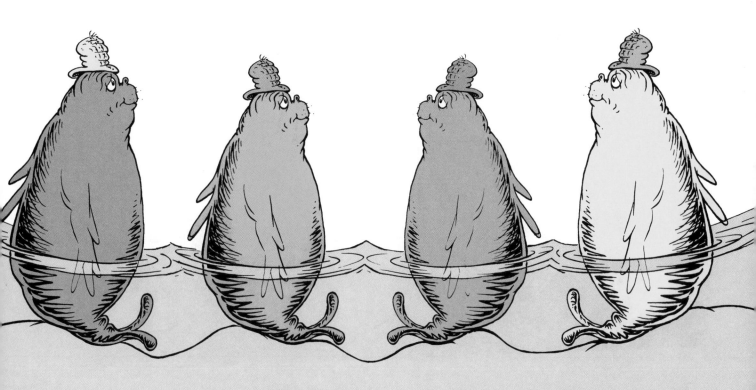

Find the sticker that goes here.

Fiffer-Feffer-Feff!

Hint: A Fiffer-Feffer-Feff has four feathers.

BIG G

little g

What can you say that begins with G?

Gooey goo is good for Goo-Geese.

How fast can you say
this G word?

goggles

Find the sticker that goes here.

alligator

box

Find the sticker that goes here.

camel

Find the sticker that goes here.

duck

egg

Find the sticker that goes here.

fish

glove

Oh, the things you can say from A to G!

BIG H
little h

What can you say that begins with H?
Henry's hinkle-horns hang on hooks.

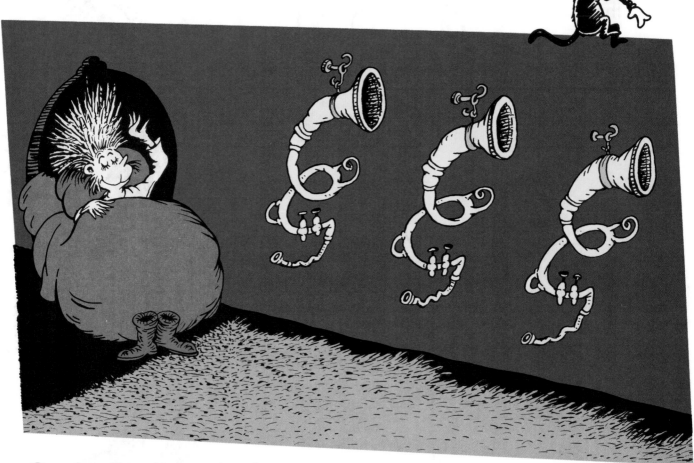

Circle the H word.

wake   bed   honk   goggles

BIG I

little i

What can you say that begins with I?
Icabod is itchy.

Help poor Mr. Potter, i-dotter, dot i's.

BIG J

little j

What can you say
that begins with J?
Jerry Jordan's jelly jar!

Jed!

Find the
sticker that
goes here.

Hint: A Jed has a pompom on his head.

BIG K

little k

What can you say
that begins with K?
King Kenneth's kerchoo!

Klotz!

Find the
sticker
that goes
here.

Hint: The Klotz has lots of dots.

BIG L

little l

What can you say that begins with L?

Luke likes to lick lakes.

Color the big L's the lime color.

Don't color the little l or the J.

Don't lick them either.

SUPER-DE-DOOPER FUN!

BIG M

little m

What can you say that begins with M?

Mice are mumbling in the moonlight.

Make the mice mumble.

Write little m's in the white spaces.

BIG N
little n

What can you say that begins with N?

Ned's nice new nightshirt!

Nureau!

Find the
sticker
that goes
here.

Hint: A Nureau has a white tail.

BIG O

little o

What do you know
that begins
with O?

Oscar's ostrich
oiled an owl.

Circle the O-shaped doughnuts.

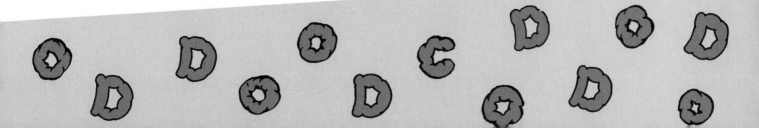

BIG P

little p

What can you say that begins with P?
Pete's a pink-pig patter.

Color the p's the pickle color.
Put blue dots on the b's.
Don't dot the d's.

b d p d b p

hat

ice

jar

Find the sticker that goes here.

kangaroo

ladder

Find the sticker that goes here.

mouse

nose

Find the sticker that goes here.

owl

Find the sticker that goes here.

pig

Oh, the things you can say from H to P!

BIG Q

little q

What can you do that begins with Q?

Quack quickly like quacker-oos.

brick   block   clock   quack

Circle the word that begins with Q.

BIG R
little r

What can you say that begins with R?

Rosy's rhinoceros is red.

Color the big R's red.
Color the little r's blue.

R R K R R R K R
r r r n r n n r

BIG S

little s

What can you say
that begins with S?
Sammy got sick
sipping sodas!

Snoo!

Find the
sticker
that goes
here.

Hint: A Snoo is blue.

BIG T

little t

What can you say that begins with T?
Ten tired turtles on a tuttle-tuttle tree!

Color the little t's green.
Color the
tuttle-tuttle tree
green too.

BIG U
little u

What can you say
that begins with U?
Uncle Ubb is under
his umbrella.

Circle the umbrella with the U-shaped handle.

BIG V

little v

What can
you say
that begins
with V?
Vera's violin
is very violet.

V V U U V U V V

Circle the V's.
Underline the U's.

BIG W

little w

What can you say that begins with W?

Watchers watch watchers watch.

What? Where? When? How?

Cross out the word that doesn't begin with W.

What is this watcher watching?

queen

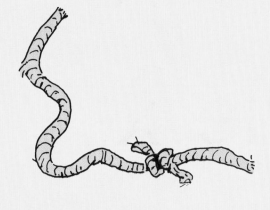

rope

Find the
sticker that
goes here.

snail

Find the
sticker that
goes here.

turtle

Find the
sticker
that goes
here.

unicorn

vase

Find the
sticker that
goes here.

walrus

Oh, the things you can say from Q to W!

BIG X

little x

What can
you say
that <u>ends</u> with X?
Knox on fox in box!

ax   box   for   fox

fix   saw   Knox   six

Cross out the words that don't end with X.

BIG Y
little y
BIG Z
little z

What can you say that begins with Y
and ends with Z?
Yolanda yells at a Zizzer-Zazzer-Zuzz!

What can you say that ends with X, Y, and Z?
The alphabet!
Write in the missing letters.

A B C D E ☐ G...
H I ☐ K L M N ☐ P...
Q ☐ S T ☐ V...
W ☐ Y and Z

Oh, the things I can say
from A to Z!
All the things in this book
were said by me!

(signed) _____